D0907272

TRANSLUCENCE

بين قارّتين

NICOLE CALLIHAN

TRANSLUCENCE

SAMAR ABDEL JABER

Book design: Sophie Appel + adam b. bohannon
Book editor: Michael Broder
Cover design: adam b. bohannon
Ms. Abdel Jaber photo: Priscilla Ainhoa Griscti
Ms. Callihan photo: Amanda Field
Published by Indolent Books,
an imprint of Indolent Arts Foundation, Inc.
www.indolentbooks.com
Brooklyn, New York
ISBN: 978-1-945023-18-7

Marry, and you will regret it; don't marry, you will also regret it; marry or don't marry, you will regret it either way. Laugh at the world's foolishness, you will regret it; weep over it, you will regret that too; laugh at the world's foolishness or weep over it, you will regret both. Believe a woman, you will regret it; believe her not, you will also regret it… Hang yourself, you will regret it; do not hang yourself, and you will regret that too; hang yourself or don't hang yourself, you'll regret it either way; whether you hang yourself or do not hang yourself, you will regret both. This, gentlemen, is the essence of all philosophy.

SØREN KIERKEGAARD

"لكنّ أحدا لا يحنُّ إلى وجع أو هلع أو جنازة. الحنين هو اختصاص الذاكرة في تجميل ما احتجب من المشهد، وترميم شبّاك سقط دون أن يصل سقوطه إلى الشارع. والحنين قصاصُ المنفى من المنفيّ، وخجل المنفيّ من الإعجاب بموسيقى منفى وحدائق. فأن تحنَّ يعني أن لا تغتبط بشيء، هنا ، إلا على استحياء .لو كنت هناك – تقول – لو كنت هناك لكانت ضحكتي أعلى وكلامي أوضح. فالحنين هو توق الكلمات إلى حيزها الأول حتى لو كانت غامضة وغريبة عن الجماعة .لكنني – تقول لنفسك – أوثر الاغتراب في المنفى على الاغتراب في البيت، ففي المنفى ما يوجب ذلك."

محمود درويش

I.

the unmoored
and the ice
and two oars
what it might mean
to disappear
into the self
into the sea
everything I never said
was true
even some I did say
the mountains
are mountains
to place
a body in this boat
would ruin it all

أحبّ البحر
وأخاف منه:
كم من غريقٍ في قاعه
أحبّ الجبال
وأخاف منها:
ثمّة رجلٌ
قطعَ يدهُ
حين علقت تحت صخرةٍ
البحار والجبال
ليست أجمل في الصّور
لكنّها أكثر أماناً
لذلك
أبتعد عنك
وأحتفظ
بصوَرك فقط

what was it I wanted
a Lebanese dinner
the snow to fall
the ache
to become apart from me
all night
I rode through the sky
holding a man's hand
which had been
cut off at the wrist
it is hard to pretend
that bodies don't matter
harder still that they do
behind a chain link fence
I wave to you

اليوم

وأنا أقود السيارة

لمعت في رأسي قصيدةٌ

ثم أخرى عند طبيب الأسنان

وواحدةٌ

في طريق العودة

الآن أجلس أمام صفحةٍ بيضاء

ولا أتذكر منها شيئاً

أحدّق في صورة بحر وشمس

وأجرّب مرّة أخرى

ثمّ أفكّر:

لماذا

ذاكرتي المثقوبة

لا تنسيني إيّاك

بنفس الطريقة؟

a perforated memory
the road
led to the road
I thought it was a dream
the clocks did the thing
clocks do
it must be tiring
to have three hands
what are all the names for
lonely
the past participle
of suffer
infinitive angst
it is embarrassing
to be this person

الطريق كانت خاليةً
إلّا من سيّارتنا
موسيقى خافتة
في الرّاديو
ونحن... إلى المجهول
يافطات بأسماء قرى
لا نعرفها
رأسي الّذي يضجّ عادةً
صامتٌ
كالجبال الجرداء المحيطة بنا
المدينة
صارت بعيدةً
يدكَ تمسك يدي
لوهلةٍ أصدّق
أنّك حقًّا لي وحدي

4.

the noises inside
my head
are mostly shadows
though a line
straight and white
ramrods my spine
some days I make
my way
to the end
of the earth
I don't mind
warm beer
or how it feels
to walk until
my legs give out

حياتي لم تكن يوماً
خطاً أبيض مستقيماً
يحيط به الضوء
لم أكن يوماً ماهرةً
في الطَّريق
كعدّاءٍ محترف
حياتي دائرة من الحزن
بلا نهاية
أزحف على أطرافها
طيلة الوقت
متى بدأ الحزن؟
أسأل نفسي
وحياتي سؤالٌ
سيظلّ
مفتوحاً إلى الأبد

but an empty boat
is not much of a boat
I am wracked
with tenderness
I could say we are all refugees
but how wrong
I would be
I would be
so wrong
the thing inside
which capsizes
all night we rode
towards the shore
and the shore
towards us

لو أنّ البحر

بقي هادئاً ذلك اليوم

لو أنّ الرّياح

أبطأت قليلاً فقط

لكانوا وصلوا:

مائةٌ وسبعة وأربعون مهاجراً

أحدٌ ما أحصاهم

واحداً واحداً

نظر إليهم

وجهاً وجهاً

وقبل أن يكتب

تقريره الصحافيّ الدقيق

أسكنهم صورةً جماعيّة

مائةٌ وسبعةٌ وأربعون

وجهاً حزيناً

6.

boats
are not the only way
to move bodies
across water
I skim the shallows
for each known thing
the fuckless days
grow quiet
my tongue as
flat and heavy
as a bloated
two by four
these houses we build
aren't built
for living

أمشي
إلى أن تخور قدماي
لكنّ البيت فارغ
ولا أودّ العودة
إلى الصّحراء
رأيت، اليوم، بيتاً
فوق نهرٍ
بين أشجارٍ شديدة الخضرة
وضبابٍ خفيف
حلمتُ أنّي أسير
على المِمر الخشبيّ
المؤدّي إليه
بينما ينتظر خطواتي
أحدٌ
ليفتح الباب

7.

the book
has all the answers
you don't feel anymore
says the book
I say okay
but what does
a book know
everything
I fall asleep
with it open
but wake
to shards of stars
and a low moan
I mistake
for my daughter

الصّحراء
تنجب هواءً حارّاً
المدينة تكفّ عن اللمعان
من فرط الغبار
صدري يضيق بي
كسجنٍ إنفرادي
فأتمرّنُ على التنفّس
عميقاً
كما علّمني الكتاب
التنفّس دواء القلق
والاكتئاب
ولا يكلّف شيئاً
هكذا يقول الكتاب
لكنّني أنسى ذلك
معظم الأحيان

8.

the least heavy
might be
the thing which is carried
always or might be
suddenly
rinsed away
blown by even
an insignificant wind
carried to sea
left on a mountain
drowned in a river
I hold so tight
to the light
that it becomes
other

في الحلم كنّا معاً
في بيتٍ كبير
وسألتك:
ماذا حلَّ بالصّوَر؟
لماذا وجهك
غريبٌ عنّي؟
حين استيقظت
وددتُ أن أراك
كان حزني شديداً
رغبت بسعادة حقيقيّة
لم أشعر بها
منذ وقتٍ طويل:
سعادة طفلةٍ
ترى البحر
للمرّة الأولى

9.

legs
thin as reeds
a snake in the water
I've been dreaming again
in dreams I am salt
and you are salt
there is no dissolution
a glass
of water
to keep by the sink
gulp greedily
the birds are so pink
you stink
of your loneliness
do I

الأحلام
تعكس حياتنا
التي لا تلتقطها الكاميرات
بخلاف طيور الفلامنجو
على مياه بحيرة الملح
رأيتك منذ قليل
أردت أن أبكي
فهربت
إلى البحيرة
لكنّي تخيّلت الملح
آثار دموعٍ
وطيور الفلامينجو
عشّاقاً
تكسّرت قلوبهم
في حياةٍ سابقة

10.

how it feels to be
washed and washed
up and out
in the rain
I watch the boats
and smoke
I might float
into the ceiling's orb
but there is no ceiling
unless you count
the sky
but no one counts
the sky do they
if so is the answer
ever one

أتشبّث بالضوء
بسحابةٍ بيضاء
بشجرةٍ ياسمين
لأطرد حلماً
رافقني طيلة اليوم
لكنّني أتذكر
صورتي في المرآة
رماديّةً، إذ أرى
بيتاً تملأ حيطانَه
بقايا الرصاص
بينما صوت أم كلثوم
في الراديو
يدّعي سلاماً
مع النفس

II.

the dream stays
with me and I stay
with the dream
an abandoned house
that which was once
inhabited inhabits me
a busted window
is less window than
hole
if all night we walk
through past rooms
where are we
when we wake
tell me how much
the shadow weighs

البيوت المهجورة
صامتةٌ طيلة الوقت
غارقةٌ في ذكريات
من كانوا سكّانها
تفتقد الأثاث، المدفأة،
المكتبة، المروحة،
وخطوات أصحابها
البيوت المهجورة
معلَّقة
بين الحياة والموت
تتأمّل منازل الآخرين
من حفرٍ في الحيطان
كانت تسمّى شبابيك
وتعيش انتظاراً
بلا نهاية

2

١.

هباء. كلّ ما قرأته هباء. التركيز الكامل للذهن؟ العيش في اللّحظة الرّاهنة؟. كلّه هباء. مثلي كمثل الفتاة في الصّورة، كمثل طاولةٍ عليها كلّ ما حلمت به. أشيح بوجهي عنها حزينةً. ليس هذا ما أريد. كلّ شيءٍ هباء. أمس فكّرت طويلاً بالمطر. كيف كانت الأرض حين هطل للمرّة الأولى؟. أغمضت عينيّ وتنشّقت الرّائحة. فكّرت بالتّفاح: كيف كان طعم التفاحة الأولى؟. فكّرت بإحساسنا الأوّل بالأشياء. حاولت تذكر المرّة الأخيرة الّتي فعلت فيها شيئاً ما للمرّة الأولى. بضع سنوات على الأرجح؟. حسناً ماذا كنت أفعل كلّ هذا الوقت؟ كيف أستعيد كلّ هذا العمر؟ وكيف أمنع هباءً سوف يأتي؟ أقرأ وأقرأ وأقرأ وأفكّر وأفكّر وأفكّر. أحلّق داخل غيمةٍ لا تعرف كيف وجدت وإلى أين تمضي. أطير أعلى وأعلى أحياناً، دون إرادتي. وأتعثّر ثمّ أسقط ثمّ أعلو. مثلي كمثل الفتاة في الصّورة، لا قول لي في ما أرى أمامي. ولا حياة داخل حياتي. أفكّر وأفكّر وأقول «اللحظة هي كلّ شيء». أقتلع دماغي. أتلو عليه، مراراً، ذلك كلّه. أعجنه، بيديّ الإثنتين، ليستجيب. لكنّي أسمعه، يهمس، من أعماقه: هباء. كلّ هذا هباء.

In order to enter the domestic sphere, you must leave the foreign. You must lock yourself in a home for eighty years and eighty nights. This is only the beginning. Here, you can refer to your body as a wound; here, your wound is all you have. There are no coordinates, only your self-made crown and a hunk of watermelon you will eat to the rind. Four apples. Three pears. Two forks, neither of which you know how to use. When I was twenty-three, S asked if I was embarrassed to not know how to use chopsticks. The yolks are broken. All night, I stare into the eye of the fish and it into me. Ella presents me with a silver box, and inside the silver box, a golden key. It opens nothing, she tells me.

2.

سيجارة حشيشٍ واحدة لا تكفي. تلزمك اثنتان على الأقل. خدرٌ طفيف في الأطراف. الغرائز تكسر أقفالها وتهرب. الحواس تحتدّ فترى أعمقَ، وقد تسمع نملةً تمشي في طرف الغرفة. أمّا التذوّق، فسيّد الحواس: الفاكهة أشهى من أيّ وقتٍ. والشوكولا عذبةٌ في الفم فلا تريد انتهاءها. ضميرك، الذي كان يمنع السكّر عنك، يحاول أن يقول شيئاً من دون جدوى. رغبات الجسد أقوى. تنفتح في دماغك أبوابٌ بلا نهاية: تذَكُّر تفاصيلٍ لم تكن تدرك أنّها ما زالت. وسموٌّ في الخيال نحو زوايا في الكون لم تصلها من قبل. الوقت طويلٌ طويل. ولا بدّ من قلقٍ خفيفٍ من أشياء كان عليك أن تفعلها. ندمٌ طفيفٌ على اتصالات لم تجبها. الجسد أكثر خمولاً وأكثر سعادةً في آنٍ معاً: الألم، الذي رافقك طيلة اليوم، حمل أمتعته ومضى. رغبةٌ بالبقاء هكذا إلى الأبد. لكن سيجارة واحدة لا تكفي. خصوصاً لو أدركت أنّه، في مكانٍ آخر، ثمّة رجلٌ في المقهى يحمل زجاجة الحليب لابنته الرضيعة، ويتحدّث مع آخر بينما يحتسيان البيرة. وكلبٌ يستمتع بشمس تمّوز. وطفلةٌ سمراء تتوقّف عن الكلام مذهولةً بغريبٍ توقّف كي يلتقط لهم صورة. سيجارة واحدة لا تكفي. خصوصاً حين تدرك أنّ ثمّة عالماً يحدث في الخارج. بينما وحدك، في غرفةٍ معتمة، تدفن آلامك، مدّعياً أنّ سيجارتين تكفيان لكي لا تبالي بذلك كلّه.

Open. The store is open. The door is open. The child is open. The baby's mouth is open, and in the mouth, milk drips from the opening of a bottle. The man on the yellow chair is not the same man as the man on the black chair, but the universe don't care. If I insert enough plastic cards into enough plastic machines, I might get enough paper to have everything I want. Desires include: a slush puppy, a beer, boundless love. The body is ridiculous and wheeling towards death, but once it was small enough to be wholly held. The bodega men are both like and unlike God; I am both like and unlike the bodega men. Of the shading in the Venn Diagram, I can only say I thought I was supposed to stick my finger in it. Two blocks away, my daughter is being scratched by a rabbit named The Professor. I won't know anything for hours.

3.

اليوم رأيت فراشة برتقالية وسوداء بنقاط بيضاء كزهورٍ مشذّبةٍ بعناية. أحدهم قال إنّ ذاك صنع الله، وإلّا كيف كلّ تلك التفاصيل! كيف كل هذه الدقّةِ!. انظروا، إنها لوحة!. آخرُ قال: إنّها صنع التطوّر، فالبرتقالي والأسود رمزا الخطر في عالم الحيوانات، وفي ألوانها سمومٌ تقتل من يحاول التهامها من العصافير. أحدهم أضاف: لماذا لا يكون الله الّذي خلق التطوّر الّذي صنع الفراشة ولوّنها؟ كنت على وشك أن أسأل: لكن من خلق الله الّذي خلق التطور الّذي صنع الفراشة؟ لكنّي التزمت الصّمت. بحثت عن اسم الفراشة بالعربية ولم أصل. حدقت في ألوانها. برتقالية وسوداء بنقاط بيضاء. ترى هل تدرك الفراشة ألوانها؟ هل، حين تحطّ قرب نافذةٍ، تنظر إلى نفسها في الزجاج وتدرك أنّها هي؟ أم تظنّ أنْ لا صلة لها بانعكاسها؟ هل، حين تصحو في الصّباح، تطير بسهولةٍ؟ أم أنّها تشعر، مثلي، بثقل أجنحتها، فتحثّ نفسها بصعوبةٍ على النهوض؟ هل تسأل نفسها مئات الأسئلة كلّ يوم؟ هل تفكّر بمعضلة الوجود؟ وهل تدرك أنّها محطّ نقاشنا، الآنَ، حول أصل الخلق؟ كنت على وشك أن أصرّح بكلّ ذلك، لكنّني، فقط، قلت: إنها جميلة.. حقاً جميلة.

And though, with our finest knife, we tore jagged holes into the metal lid; and though, with our six hands, mine veiny, and my daughters' small and nail-bitten, we ripped sweet grasses from the earth and made a bed of those sweet grasses inside the jar; and though we dug through the medicine cabinet, beyond the Benadryl and the foot balm, the concealer purchased at an Oklahoma Rite-Aid in 2002, the Children's Claritin, the unicorn sparkle lotion, the spools and spools of floss, all in search of an eyedropper in which we would place the sugar-water that we mixed in a small bowl in the afternoon light of the kitchen; and though, yes, we even lifted its name in prayer, our caterpillar died.

4.

يحلو لي أن أصدّق أننا، بعد الموت، نصير غيوماً شديدة البياض، تسوح في العالم بحريّة مطلقة: لا مطارات ولا جوازات سفر ولا تأشيرات. يحلو لي أن أصدّق أنّ الله مات في عمر الثمانين، وتركنا وحدنا دون إرادته. وإلّا كيف كلّ هذه الفوضى! كيف كلّ هذا الخراب!. يحلو لي أن أصدّق أنّ الموت أكثر رحمةً من الحياة. وأنّنا، إن دفنّا أو حُرقنا، لا ندرك ذلك حقّاً. يحلو لي أن أصدّق أنّ قلوبنا، تحت التّراب، تصبح جذورَ زهور حمراء حمراء فوق التراب. يحلو لي أن أصدّق أنّ الحياة برنامج كاميرا خفيّة. وأنّ المذيع سيظهر عمّا قريبٍ مع الله. سينهض المرضى من أسرّتهم، والأموات من قبورهم. ونضحك نضحك نضحك كلّنا معاً إلى الأبد. يحلو لي أن أصدّق أنّ للأبد نهايةً يختارها من يشاء لنفسه متى يشاء. يحلو لي أن أصدّق أنّنا، بعد الموت، سنكون كأنّنا لم نولد. وأنّنا قبل الموت، ولو بلحظة واحدة، سوف ندرك مغزى الحياة! يحلو لي أن أتوقّف عن كلّ ذلك الآن. أن أعود عشرين عاماً إلى الوراء، أتصفّح مجلّة سطحيّةً في صالون السّيدات، في انتظار أن تنتهي أمّي لتأخذني إلى محلّ الألعاب.

Is the bottle in which my blonde is held the same bottle which holds my mother's blonde? Is the lemon juice that I squeezed into my teenage strands as I sat on a strip of teenage sand the same lemon juice that my daughters will squeeze into their teenage strands? Can you die of vanity? (I might.) A bottle is a bottle is a bottle. If the brain could be dug from the head, would it be ashamed of its nasolabial folds? Confession: I stayed up all night plucking my grays. Question: if what is real is X, how close can you get to Y while still maintaining your X-ness? Zzzz… In Santiago, a poet says: rubia, rubia, rubia. In the middle of China, I ride a rickshaw and let a boy touch my hair.

5.

كان عليك أن تحدّق جيّداً في عينيّ الغزال الواسعتين قبل أن تطلق النار. عينان سوداوان تحاولان التقاط عينيك لإرسال نظرة حزن، كأنّهما تدركان ما سوف يحدث بعد قليل. وويكيبيديا تقول إنّك تستطيع أخذ اللحم لصنع وجبةٍ شهيّةٍ، والجلد لصنع ثيابٍ للجسد، والقرون لصنع مقابض للسكاكين. وحدها العيون تبقى كما هي إذن. تقول أيضاً، ويكيبيديا، إنّ اصطياد الغزلان رياضةٌ شائعة. أفكّر بالعينين السّوداوين. أغمض عينيّ وأحدّق فيهما. أقرأ فيهما مئة قصيدة هايكو، أسافر إلى اليابان، إلى كيوتو، أسير في مرجٍ تملأ أرضَه بتلاتُ الورود الملوّنة: صفراء، حمراء، زهريّة، بيضاء فوق عشبٍ أخضر. أركض مع الغزال حتّى أتعب. ثمّ أحدّق في عينيه.. تُرى هل يبكي مثلنا حين يحزن؟ هل يخاف الموت؟ هل يصيبه قلق الآتي؟ هل يكتئب أحيانا؟ هل يتساءل بمَ أفكّر أنا الآن؟ وويكيبيديا لا تُشبع أسئلتي. أغمض عينيّ.. أقترب منه.. الرّصاصة تخترق جسده، وعيناهُ نظرةٌ حزينةٌ إلى الأبد.

Friday. July. I have gotten out of bed, and though I should be confronting my demons (or, at least, cleaning something, emailing someone), I stare instead at a photograph of a baby deer. I would like to rub the softness of its ear. I would like to have a whole garden of lamb's ears and for the years to be less like years. I would like summer squash, and to not be lonely, or to be lonelier. The body is grass and bruises, a collection of what it has and/or hasn't consumed. On Saturday, we wrapped the dead rabbit in a soft cloth. My husband hung the American flag above the garage. The girls burned their marshmallows, and we told them they were better that way. O tongue, you are a dirty thing.

6.

حين أبلغ الستّين سوف أسافر إلى مكانٍ لا يعرفني فيه أحد، أرتدي فستاناً بلون الفوشيا وأغنّي بصوتٍ عالٍ في الطَّريق. سوف أصنع بالوناً من العلكة وأفرقعه في المصعد بين بضعة غرباء. سوف أقود السّيارة بتهوّرٍ بعد أن أشرب زجاجة نبيذٍ كاملة. سوف أذهب إلى مدينة الملاهي وألعب عن كلّ تلك السّنوات الهزيلة الّتي أمضيتها خلف المكاتب. سوف أوزّع الأموال في الشوارع على الأطفال الجائعين وألتقط صوراً لابتساماتهم. سوف أشتري بيانو وأتدرّب على معزوفةٍ واحدةٍ حتّى أتقنها، وأعزفها أمام الأصدقاء في كلّ السّهرات. سوف أقول «لا» بكثرةٍ دون تبرير. سوف أرمي هاتفي في البحر، واللابتوب من النافذة. سوف أقرأ مكتبتي كلّها. سوف أمضي ليلةً كاملةً على الشاطئ وحدي، أنصت إلى صوت الموج فقط. سوف أستأجر كوخاً في غابةٍ بعيدة وأزاول التأمّل أسبوعاً كاملاً. سوف أكتب سيرتي الشخصيّة. سوف أقفز من طائرةٍ وأترك حياتي رهن المظلّة لبضع ثوانٍ. سوف أحفظ كلّ أغاني نينا سيمون وفرانك سيناترا. سوف أشاهد فيلم «أميلي» عشر مرّاتٍ متواصلة. سوف أشاهد «جيم أوف ثرونز». سوف أقرأ «ألف ليلة وليلة». سوف أحفظ ديوان المتنبّي. وبعد كلّ ذلك، سوف أذهب إلى فلسطين وأبقى هناك، إلى الأبد، بطريقةٍ غير شرعيّة!

On Fire Island, the boys spool out yards and yards of twine. *To measure the sea*, they say. The anchored boats hold no bodies. Everything is as empty as I am. In a borrowed cup, bitter coffee grows cold. Afternoons, the girls walk to the store to buy too much gum to blow too big bubbles. Evenings, I comb pink out of their lashes. Eva sits with me, asks me to write about her. *What do you want me to say?* I don't say. *That I will kill anyone who brings you harm? That I will break every single bone in the hand of anyone who touches you against your will?* But she only wants Corn Flakes, and for me to tell you who has come across this poem that she is awesome, that she has a scratch on her face that her sister gave her on the ferry, that she likes to do cartwheels. I number my shames to seven and make a scavenger hunt for the children. What is the opposite of opposite? Storm is to storm as you are to you, as home is to home, thumbtack to thumbtack, thigh to thigh, eye to eye. Let's have a heart to heart. O how big is this sea.

7.

أدلّك العضلات الّتي تؤلمني، فتؤلمني أكثر. الجسد، إن لم يقتله سببٌ خارجيّ، يقتل نفسه بنفسه الجسد، بعد الثلاثين، يصبح متّصلاً بالرّوح أكثر. يمرضان معاً، يسترجعان الحياة معاً، وفي النهاية يموتان معاً. تقول لي يارا: لي صديقة اخترعتها، أخبرها كلّ أسراري. أقول لها: وأنا كان عندي صديق متخيّل حين كنت في عمرك. أحاول أن أتذكّر متى نسيته. متى كانت المرّة الأخيرة الّتي تحدّثنا فيها؟ أناديه باسمه الّذي اخترعته طفلةً، لكنّه لا يستجيب. تُرى هل يكون قد رآني صامتةً فارتحل إلى جسدٍ آخر. هل يكون قد مات، وما أعيشه من حزنٍ دائم هو حدادي المتواصل عليه؟. عضلاتي شديدة التشنّج الآن. المسكّن لا ينفع ولا الكمّادات السّاخنة تشفي. الألم يتسلّق جسدي. أشعر أنّي أصعد درجاً دائرياً طويلاً يمتدّ إلى ما لا نهاية. نفسي يكاد ينقطع. أحاول أن أحبّ جسدي، أن أحتضن الألم، بدل أن أعامله كعدوٍّ كما تعوّدت. إنّها الواحدة بعد منتصف الليل. لا بدّ أنّ يارا تغرق الآن في النوم. أحاول أن أتذكّر صوت صديق الطفولة الخيالي. هل كان صوته صوتي؟ هل فقدني ففقدته؟ أصرخ باسمه في داخلي. لكن لا جواب.

Also, there was a snail. If we let it go before or after it died doesn't seem to matter. The spiral of its shell. Fingerprints on glass. Fungus under a nail. Jane says: the rain brought the bugs. I wake in the middle of the night and walk the planks above the bay. A searchlight searches for something. It is not unusual to think about dying. Other things that are not unusual to think about: desire, candy corn, the boy with the acne. The children say your heart stops beating when you sneeze. But I think this is wrong. The weatherman says the worst is over. I think this is wrong too. The stairs are deep and wide. A man's hand reaches for a lemon in a bowl, cuts it in half with a knife. The body is too often a disappointment. At some point, you must accept the possibility that no one will ever go down on you again.

8.

يتحدّثون عن انتصاراتٍ كبيرةٍ ولا أفهم شيئاً. أفكّر بهزائمي الصّغيرة المتكرّرة. أقرأ خبراً عن كوكبٍ تمّ اكتشافه حديثاً. أغوص في كونيَ الداخلي الذي لم يصله أحدٌ غيري. يكتبون مواقفهم من كلّ شيء، وأعجز عن اتّخاذ موقفٍ واحدٍ! العالم يسير بسرعةٍ لا أستطيع مجاراتها. أشعر طيلة الوقت أنّي في دوّامةٍ تدور وتدور وتدور أسرع من أن أدرك أيّ شيء. كلّ جوابٍ وجدته صار سؤالاً. وكلّ سؤالٍ لم أستطع الإجابة عليه أنجب مئات الأسئلة. كلّ كتابٍ قرأته أوصلني إلى كتابٍ لم أقرأه. وكلّ كتابٍ لم أقرأه يذكّرني أنّ الموت آتٍ لا محالة. أحياناً، أشعر أنّ الأبديّة، كاملةً، لن تكفيَ لأكتب ما أودّ قوله. لكنّي، معظم الوقت، أجلس برأسٍ فارغة أمام صفحة فارغة. أشعر لثوانٍ بجدواي، وباللاجدوى طيلة الوقت. أحاول أن أفهم، فأشعر أنّي في متاهةٍ كلّما اقتربت من نهايتها، ابتعدت. السّاعة الخامسة بعد الظّهر. أضع الكنبة أمام الواجهة الزجاجية وأحدّق في الأفق. الأشجار لا تتحرّك. الهواء منعدمٌ في الخارج. المشهد أشبه بلوحةٍ لولا حركة السّيارات الّتي تعبر. أحتاج فقط أن أعانقك وأغفوَ طويلاً.

You are thirteen again, and you are writing every thought you have into a journal. You want your mother to die; you want your mother to live forever. You want to die; you want to live forever. Tina Ramsey is fat; Tina Ramsey is a bitch. Tina Ramsey is a BIG FAT BITCH; you would give any of several organs to trade lives with Tina Ramsey. Heart doodle. Sad face doodle. Bullet in the brain doodle. Happy face. Doodle doodle. What rhymes with noodle? Cockadoodle. Cockamamie. Cocked gun. Cocked jaw. Weird flesh in your hand for those eternal seven minutes in a closet. *In lieu of flowers*, your daughter will eventually write, *please cast your old blue sweaters to the fishes.*

9.

تسألينني كيف التخلّص من الخوف، ولا أعرف ماذا أجيبك. أنا عالقةٌ أيضاً يا صديقتي، لكن يحلو لي
أن أصدّق أنّ الخوف سيكون رفيقنا في الثلاثينيّات فقط، كما كان الارتباك رفيقنا في العشرينيّات. لا
بدّ سنشعر، فجأةً، حين نطأ الأربعين، بسلام داخليٍّ كما لو أنّنا دخلنا مدينةً جديدة، وسنصبح فجأةً
حكماء، نعطي الأجيال التالية دروساً قيّمةً في الحياة. كنت أقرأ مقالاً للتوّ عن السّعادة، يقول إنّ
علينا أن نغمض أعيننا، ونفكّر بشخصٍ غيّر حياتنا بطريقةٍ جيّدة، وأن نكتب رسالة شكرٍ له. أقلّب
الوجوه في رأسي وأختار بعضها، لكنّني لا أملك طاقةً لكتابة أيّ شيءٍ إلى أيّ أحد. هل تشعرين مثلي
بانعدام القدرة على الحياة؟ هل تشعرين مثلي بالقلق طيلة الوقت؟ هل يؤثّر الطقس في حياتك
بقدر ما يؤثّر في حياتي؟ الحرارة تكاد تصهرني. المكيّفات تزعجني وتؤلم عظامي. أشعر أنّني في سجن،
داخل قضيّةٍ منسيّةٍ لن يتغيّر فيها شيء. أودّ أن أجلس تحت شجرةٍ فيما نسيمٌ من الهواء يمرّ خفيفاً.
أن أحدّق في ظلال أوراقها على الأرض وهي تصنع أشكالاً أفسّرها كما يحلو لي. أقرأ كتاب 1984 منذ
أكثر من شهرين. لا شكّ أنّ حياة وينستون تشبه حياتي. هل تشعرين كذلك أنت أيضاً؟ أغمض عينيّ
الآن وأتذكّر لحظة سعادة. فلتفعلي ذلك أنت أيضاً. فجأةً أشعر بنوستالجيا لذيذة. سأقرأ "ذبابة في
الحساء قريباً"..

To be shadow. The shape produced by the body which comes between the rays of light and a surface. Or shadows, as beneath the eyes, as regions of opacity on a radiograph, i.e., *shadows on her lungs*. And/ or, also, to be in partial or complete darkness, especially as produced this way. See: *the north side of the cathedral deep in shadow.* See: *the mosque.* Am I a shadow of my former self? Is there anything I can claim without a shadow of doubt? At the beach, my daughters are my shadows. How can I walk off the end of the earth if they follow so closely behind? Notice, too, the jasmine flower, cast in diffuse light. By which I mean, most shadows go undetected. Years ago, I sat, reading *1984*, in the dark left by leaves. Germanic in root. From the Old English, meaning to screen or shield from attack. Few things in nature disarm as much as darkness.

I0.

تسألينني إن كنت أصلّي. فأرجع خمسة عشر عاماً إلى الوراء. حين كنت، بريئةً كالأطفال، أؤمن بالآلهة. كنت أقف على سجّادة الصّلاة بسكينةٍ أفتقدها الآن. لكنّني كنت أبالغ إذ أفكّر في جدوى ذلك، فأقلعت. تسألينني إن كنت أغطّي رأسي. لا، لا أفعل. ولا يشغل ذلك بالي حقّاً. لكنّني منذ بضعة شهورٍ لاحظت في رأسي شعرةً بيضاء واحدة. اقتلعتها فعادت. اقتلعتها فعادت. ثمّ اقتلعتها فعادت. لن أكذب عليك. شعرةٌ بيضاء واحدة أخذت حيّزاً لا بأس به من تفكيري. قولي لي كيف تتعاملين مع الشعر الأبيض؟ هل يؤرقك أن يكون مرور العمر واضحاً إلى هذه الدرجة؟ تقولين إنّكِ تكتبين من سريرٍ بين الجبال. أنا أكتب من سريرٍ في وسط الصّحراء. لكنّني في الحقيقة أقطن داخل إعلانٍ كبير. اليافطات ذات الألوان الفاقعة تحاصرني في كلّ مكان. أشكّ أحياناً كثيرة أنّني روبوت وُضِع في هذه المدينة من أجل تجربة ذكاءٍ اصطناعي، وبأنّي في النهاية، بعد أن أحقّق هدفاً معيّناً، سأحال إلى التقاعد: مجرّد آلة معطّلة. قولي لي. هل تشغل الأماكن تفكيرك؟ هل تشعرين بالانتماء حيث أنت؟ كيف تفعلين ذلك؟ هل تؤرقك أفكارٌ عن حياة بديلة؟ أنا أفكّر في فلسطين كلّ يوم. لا كقضيّة، ولا كتاريخ. أفكّر بها كمكان. الساعة الرابعة بعد الظهر. فارق التوقيت بيننا ثماني ساعات. ربّما تكونين قد استيقظت الآن.

Bear with me. Picture (though it is not to picture but to feel): a phantom limb dipped into the waters of a desert mirage. What I mean is: an ache is an ache is. Is it? Is it like the story of the famous writer who has an ingrown toenail and requests that his guest, who has flown in from Sweden, drives to Connecticut to visit him? When she arrives in a van and is wheeled out in her wheelchair, the writer remembers that the woman is paralyzed from the waist down. *You must think I'm ridiculous*, he says. *No, no*, she says. *I would imagine, if I could feel my legs, an ingrown nail would be quite cumbersome.* Perhaps, in this way, men and women are different. Or Americans and foreigners. Or everybody and everybody. I write this from a bed at the base of a mountain. I must have left my sense in the city.

II.

انتظرت رسالة منك ولم تصل. هل توافقين أن الإنتظار بات أصعب في عالمنا الإلكتروني السريع؟ قديماً كانوا ينتظرون الرسائل شهوراً. كانت البحار، حقّاً، بحاراً، والقارّات قارّات. ترى هل كانوا، مع مرور الوقت، ينسون ما كانوا ينتظرون فيصير انتظارهم أسهل؟ هل كانوا ينشغلون بعيشهم بينما ينتظرون؟ فيما نحن ننشغل بالانتظار نفسه؟ أمس، شاهدت فيلماً يحكي عن تحوّل البشر بعد قرون إلى وحوشٍ تقتات من دماء بعضها. يسمّونهم «جياعاً». ولا شكّ أنّ ثمّة بشراً أصليّين يحاولون استعادة الأرض. لكن، أليس البشر الآن وحوشاً تقتات من دماء بعضها؟ أليسوا جياعاً؟ رشاشات، وأزهار لوتس، تقولين. أليس ذلك وصفاً دقيقاً للبشر؟ رشّاشات وأزهار لوتس. رشّاشات وأزهار لوتس. أكرّرها. أتخيّلها. هكذا كنّا منذ وجود البشريّة، وهكذا سوف نستمرّ. هل توافقيني في ذلك؟ حسناً، دعينا من كلّ ذلك الآن. قولي لي. هل تحبّ ابنتك القراءة؟ الكتابة؟ هل تسألك أسئلة كثيرة عن العالم؟ لا شكّ أنّها مهمّة صعبة: أن تدّعي معرفة جميع الإجابات، أن تتصرّفي بشكلٍ صحيح طيلة الوقت، لكي تكوني مثلاً أعلى. قولي لي: كيف تستطيعين كلّ ذلك؟

To hold in the mind: machine guns and lotus flowers; the patch of sun where I could go but stay instead inside the screen, afraid of bugs, it seems; the slender bare feet of a woman I admire; the gut of her spouse. I am not sure what we are trying to do here, but you are taking shape for me. My daughter asks if I will see you when I go to the woods. *No, no,* I say. *She is in the desert. Dubai. The other side of the world.* This morning I picked a fat tick off the plastic head of a baby doll. Do you have ticks in Dubai? Do you cover your head? How often do you pray? Every night, I try a prayer with my girls. It is like water. Not meant to register. Like everything. Like nothing. *Who is Lord?* The little one asks. Yesterday, the car broke down, and while I waited for help, I lay in the grass and looked at the empty sky.

12.

ما رأيك أن نستبدل الأدوار ليومٍ واحدٍ أو شهرٍ واحد أو عامٍ كاملٍ؟ هكذا أسافر إلى حيث أنت وتأتين إلى حيث أنا. كما في تلك القصة التي قرأتها صغيرةً. أنا أُمضي الوقت مع ابنتيك، بينما تذهبين إلى عملي. أعيش فصولاً أربعة (شتاءً حقيقياً)، بينما تعيشين الجوّ الصحراوي بكامل تفاصيله. ما رأيك أن أرى بعينيّ عالمك، وترين عالمي بعينيكِ. ثمّ نعود لنكتب عن ذلك. اليوم، استيقظت حزينةً. كان ثمّة حلمٌ غير مكتمل يشدّني نحوه. حاولت التذكّر وعجزت. راودتني رغبة في الصراخ من النافذة بأعلى صوتي، لعلّ شيئاً ما يحدث. الشتاء لن يأتي. قلت ذلك لنفسي مراراً فيما هواءٌ ساخنٌ في الخارج يحرّك الأشجار الصّغيرة وينثر الغبار في كلّ مكان. أمس قرأت قصّة «التحوّل» لكافكا. هل قرأتها؟ إنها مذهلة. تخيّلي أنْ تستيقظي يوماً ما لتجدي أنّك أصبحت حشرة! حشرة في غرفة واسعة. كان ممتعاً أن أرى هموم «جريجور» تتحوّل من هموم رجلٍ إلى هموم حشرة!. سأبدأ بكتابٍ جديدٍ اليوم. يبدو ذلك الشيء الوحيد الممتع بالنسبة لي حالياً. اليوم، استيقظت حزينةً. راودتني رغبة أن أبسط حياتي أمام أحدٍ غيري. أن أقول بكلّ صراحةٍ: لقد عجزت عن إصلاحها. فلتحاول أنت!

In the country, my daughters drop a farm egg into a jar of white vinegar and call it an experiment. Beyond the trees, a storm builds, and waiting for something to happen, we pass the hours reading a How-to-do-Everything book: how to banish imaginary monsters, prune a rosebush, rim a glass with salt. I have been trying not to drink too much. How to fake an exposed bone, fit out a foxhole radio, tell time with a potato. The book recommends folding panties in thirds for travel; harnessing a cloud's power; adorning bouquets with satin ribbon. There's a two-page spread on how to identify male facial hair. How to cut a mango, walk safely in a swamp, disarm a homemade bomb. My husband says he can hear me ticking. I imagine him sticking his fingers inside me to try to find the right wire to cut.

13.

هل تصدّقين أنَّني لم أفكّر أبداً بالكسوف؟ أم لعلّي فعلت ذلك صغيرةً، حين كانت الدهشة طازجةً، ونسيت؟ أعني أنَّني، الآن، مستغربة أنَّ حدثاً بتلك الضخامة، بهذا التعقيد، لا يأخذ أيّ حيّز من اهتمامي. أعتقد أنَّنا، إذ نجاوز الثلاثين، نتعامل مع العالم كشيء مسلَّم به فنكفّ عن الاندهاش. هل فعلاً يحدث ذلك بعد الثلاثين؟ أم أنَّ ذلك يحدث لي أنا فقط؟ هل عليّ أن أكفّ عن تفسير الأشياء والمشاعر على أنَّها مرتبطة بعمر معيّن؟ أمس قامت أمّي، بيدها التي كسرت منذ بضعة أسابيع، لتصنع لي كوباً من الحليب. أليس ذلك الحبّ بعينه؟. أبي، في الطريق إلى البيت، سألني أيّ نوعٍ من البيرة أريد، وفتح الزجاجة لي. سامي قبَّلني عشر مرّات خلال اليوم. ويارا أصرّت أن تنام إلى جانبي. يربكني كلّ هذا الحبِّ، ولا أفهم كيف أنسى كلَّ ذلك حين أسافر. كيف يعجنني الروتين بشكلٍ يومي ليجرّدني من كلّ شيء، من كلّ شيء!. أعجز عن السعادة الآن لخوفي من افتقاد كلّ ذلك. لاحقاً أعجز عن السّعادة لأسبابٍ أخرى. دائماً أعجز عن السّعادة!. السّماء رماديّة رغم أنَّنا في آب. أشعر برغبة شديدةٍ لترك هاتفي في المنزل والذّهاب إلى الغابة القريبة. أمس، قال الطبيب «تأمّلي نملة تمشي في الأرض. تصعد وتهبط وتصعد وتهبط.. انسي كلَّ شيءٍ آخر وتأمّلي نملة».

50

Eva says the eclipse makes her feel guilty. Bodies in front of bodies. Bodies between bodies. Bodies on bodies. O body, I dreamed I dragged a bucket across the desert and tried to drown you. All week I have been itching. Twice, my friend has checked me for lice, and twice she has found nothing. I feel guilty about everything: the strawberry jelly I let my daughter eat from the jar, last night's falling star, the rice, the rain, the funeral parlor, hating the sound of words coming out of mouths, the crush I had on a boy who thumbtacked a Dixie flag above the dirty sheets of his never-made waterbed. How long does it take for one self to eclipse the other? Self as woman at kitchen table, as thief, whore, white trash, hick, bitch. Self in bed. Tea, honey, wine. Dirt, air, pine.

14.

أحتاج تطبيقاً يوازن الدوبامين والسيروتونين في الدماغ. أحتاج تطبيقاً يصنع غيوماً ثمّ مطراً في المدينة الحارّة. أحتاج تطبيقاً ينقلني عشرة أعوام إلى الوراء. أحتاج تطبيقاً يمنع السيناريوهات الأسوأ من احتلال دماغي طيلة الوقت. أحتاج تطبيقاً يعلّمني العيش من غير حب. أحتاج تطبيقاً يعلّمني العيش مع الحب. أحتاج تطبيقاً يزرع شجرةً وسط الصحراء ثمّ يغطيها بالثّلج. أحتاج تطبيقاً يضخّ هواءً نقيّاً نقيّاً. أحتاج تطبيقاً يستأصل رغبتي بالبكاء. أحتاج تطبيقاً ينجب لي ولداً. أحتاج تطبيقاً يمنحني ثقة المؤمنين. أحتاج تطبيقاً يمنحني ثقة الملحدين. أحتاج تطبيقاً ينقلني إلى مدينةٍ جديدةٍ كلّما مللت. أحتاج تطبيقاً يمحو حاجتي للانتماء إلى شخصٍ أو مكان. أحتاج تطبيقاً يعطيني ما لا أملك لأدرك أنّه ليس حقّاً ما أريد. أحتاج تطبيقاً يصلح يد أمّي المكسورة ويخفض السّكر عند أبي خلال ثوانٍ. أحتاج تطبيقاً يذكرني بالانهيار بوجود الشمس. أحتاج تطبيقاً يمنحني نوماً عميقاً خالياً من صرير الأسنان. أحتاج تطبيقاً يعيد لي ما نسيت. أحتاج تطبيقاً يرجع جدّي وجدّتي إلى الحياة. أحتاج تطبيقاً يضخّ سعادةً عند الاستيقاظ. أحتاج تطبيقاً يعيدني إلى عام 1948 ويغيّر التاريخ.

I read a story once of a mother who, with a broken hand, went into her kitchen in the desert to warm a cup of milk for her grown daughter. Do you know it? Or the one of the man in China who could not bear the sound of his wife's chopsticks knocking against the bowl when she ate her morning rice? A sore on the spine. I have put away ten thousand spoons since I met you. Or the same spoon ten thousand times. Or five spoons each two thousand times. Ten, one. Have I changed? Do we ever? Ever not? Evergreen. Nevermind. This is the story of a straight white line, the story of animals that are blind, of bodies in boats, of the statue that was felled, of my flag and your flag, your father and mine. It might as well be 1949. To ourselves we must be kind.

ABOUT THE AUTHORS

NICOLE CALLIHAN is the author of *Henry River Mill Village* (Arcadia Publishing, 2012), co-authored with Ruby Young Kellar; the poetry collection *SuperLoop* (Sock Monkey Press, 2014); and the poetry chapbooks: *A Study in Spring* (Rabbit Catastrophe Press, 2015), co-authored Zoë Ryder White and winner of the Baltic Writing Residency Chapbook Contest Award; *The Deeply Flawed Human* (Deadly Chaps Press, 2016); *Downtown* (Finishing Line Press 2017); and *Aging* (Yes, Poetry, 2018). Callihan is assistant director and senior language lecturer at the New York University Tandon School of Engineering, and lives in Brooklyn.

SAMAR ABDEL JABER is the author of *Wa fi rewayaten okhra (And There Are Other Accounts*; Malameh Publishing House, 2008), *Madha law konna ashbahan (What If We Were Ghosts*; Dar al-Ahlia Publishing, 2013), winner of the Palestinian Young Writer of the Year Award from the A.M. Qattan Foundation, and *Kawkab mansey (The Forgotten Planet*; Dar al-Ahlia Publishing, 2016). Abdel Jaber was recognize by the Danish Institute in Damascus for the best poems that reflect the status of Arab societies after the Arab Spring and its effect on youth. Abdel Jaber holds a bachelor's degree from Beirut Arab University and currently works in Dubai.

ABOUT INDOLENT BOOKS

INDOLENT BOOKS is a small nonprofit poetry press founded in 2015 and operating in Brooklyn, N.Y. Indolent publishes poetry by underrepresented voices whose work is innovative, provocative, and risky, and that uses all the resources of poetry to address urgent racial, social, and economic justice issues and themes.

Web: indolentbooks.com
Instagram: @indolent_books
Twitter: @IndolentBooks

CPSIA information can be obtained
at www.ICGtesting.com
Printed in the USA
BVHW04s1917110518
516028BV00001B/8/P